The
CONOCO
Collector's Bible

With Values

TODD P. HELMS

Schiffer Publishing Ltd

77 Lower Valley Road, Atglen, PA 19310

DEDICATION

This book is dedicated to my loving wife, Rebecca.
Without her patience and undying support, a man like
myself would not have been able to pursue this hobby
with child-like enthusiasm.

Library of Congress Cataloging-in-Publication Data

Helms, Todd.
The Conoco collector's bible / Todd Helms
p.   cm.
Includes bibliographical references.
ISBN: 0-88740-837-0 (paper)
1, Continental Oil Company--Collectibles--Catalogs. 2. Petroleum
industry and trade--United States--Collectibles--Catalogs
I. Title.
NK808.H36   1995
338.7'6223382'0973--dc20   95-5802
CIP

ISBN: 0-88740-837-0

Printed in China.

We are interested in hearing from authors with
book ideas on related topics.

Published by Schiffer Publishing Ltd.
77 Lower Valley Road
Atglen, PA 19310
Please write for a free catalog.
This book may be purchased from the publisher.
Please include $2.95 for postage.
Try your bookstore first.

CONTENTS

ACKNOWLEDGMENTS

It always amazes me how friendly and open people are when I talk to them about Conoco history or memorabilia. These are the people who made this book possible.

I would like to thank Jim Matthews in the Corpus Christi Conoco Office for the use of his library of *Red Triangle* magazines.

I wish to thank Conoco retiree John Beltz and his wife for inspiring me to write this book. Mr. and Mrs. Beltz took me into their home and shared with me their fond memories of Conoco.

I also wish to thank Conoco retiree Bert Striegler for his help on Conoco motor oil history and his donation of some personal pieces to my collection.

Thanks to Charles Plant of Creative Services for his photography and layout work.

My sincere gratitude to Conoco and its employees for their support in this project.

Above all, I want to thank the Lord, our God. Without Him, nothing would be possible.

Hottest Brand Going!

CONOCO

**Meet the man behind the brand—
for service with that Conoco plus!**

You get all the expected attention, and more besides when you stop at a Conoco station. Every time you drive in, busy Conoco hands are quick to clean your windshield from corner to corner—clean your back and side windows, too, if they need it—check your tires, battery and water—sweep your floorboards, if you wish. Service like this helps keep Conoco the hottest brand going!

54a

INTRODUCTION

Several years ago, I began working for a small major oil company, Conoco, in Corpus Christi, Texas. By chance, I stumbled onto some old Conoco advertisements from *The Saturday Evening Post* in a local antique shop. My life has not been the same since.

That meager purchase was the beginning of my passion for collecting Conoco memorabilia. Unlike some collectors, however, I was not satisfied with just buying collectibles, I wanted to know the history behind each piece I bought. This quest for knowledge sparked my desire to compile this book. I have received so much enjoyment meeting people and tracking down this information that I wanted to share it with others. Likewise, I hope those who read this book will be willing to share the knowledge they gain while collecting with others like myself.

For those of you who do not consider yourselves collectors yet, there are less of you now than there were a few years ago. This hobby has enjoyed a healthy period of growth for people of all ages. Oil and gas memorabilia collecting has developed into a great way to invest time and money into items and memories from an era never to be repeated.

Most of this book deals with Conoco memorabilia from 1929 to around 1970, when the Continen-

tal Oil Company used its popular triangle trademark. There are two reasons for this. First, prior to 1929, Conoco used the sentinel logo. Most collectibles with this logo are relatively expensive and more difficult to find. Second, less historical data is available for the pre-1929 items.

I have done extensive research to gather most of this information. To the best of my knowledge, all data enclosed in these pages is accurate. I would appreciate information from the reader if that is not the case. Most of this information was uncovered through Conoco company archives, current Conoco employees, other collectors, several Conoco retirees, and various pieces of literature.

I have included general pricing guidelines for the collectibles shown in this book. The actual value of any item varies depending on condition, quality, geographic location, and rarity. The combination of these factors makes it impossible to create a truly accurate value for each item. I can, however, offer a price guide based on what one would realistically expect to pay at retail or auction. Please understand that these prices are only guidelines and the author accepts no responsibility for loss or gain the reader may experience as a result of using the listed values.

Continental Oil Company (Conoco) is possibly the oldest major oil company founded in the United States still operating under its original name. Continental Oil and Transportation Company was founded on November 25, 1875 by Issac Blake in Ogden, Utah. It was during this time of massive growth in the West that Conoco began to flourish and build its marketing expertise. During the next thirty to forty years, the United States left the horse and buggy behind and began its love affair with the automobile.

The first edition of *The Conoco Magazine,* dated July 1929, announcing the merger of Conoco and Marland.

In 1908, a Pennsylvania geologist by the name of Ernest Whitworth (E.W.) Marland moved to Ponca City, Oklahoma. Marland began many exploration and production ventures, and in 1917 Marland Oil and Refining Company was founded. Marland Oils soon took the exploration, production, and refining world by storm.

Marland Oil Company purchased the Continental Oil Company in April 1929. Strangely enough, Marland decided to keep the Conoco name. Many seem to think this was because of Conoco's strong marketing presence. Regardless of the reasoning, what developed was a strong, diverse petroleum company that has been operating for 120 years.

As a result of the merger, the Continental Oil Company of today emerged. The old Continental Oil Company headquarters had been Denver, Colorado, and the Marland headquarters had been New York City, New York. Ponca City, Oklahoma was chosen to be the new company headquarters. It was sometime later that Conoco relocated its headquarters to its present location, Houston, Texas. The trademark of the new company became the combination of the Marland triangle logo with the Conoco name attached. This new symbol was used on Conoco stations and products from 1929 until the early 1970s, when the modern day Conoco capsule was adopted.

This book will concentrate on the fifty year period from the 1920s through the 1970s. We will explore the products, stations, and advertising of this period in Conoco's history. The rest of this chapter is devoted to photographs of stations and station attendants from these years. Not only are these photos fun to look at, but they are also useful tools to use when dating items or identifying items missing from your collection.

Location unknown (1936).

Attendant maintaining pumps at a 1936 station.

Location unknown (notice Germ Processed can display, 1936).

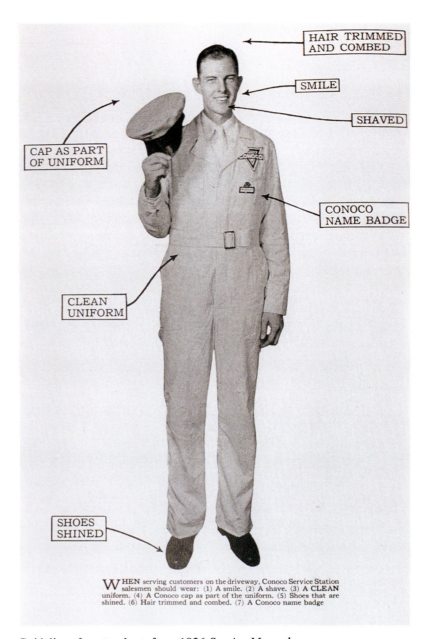

HAIR TRIMMED AND COMBED

SMILE

SHAVED

CAP AS PART OF UNIFORM

CONOCO NAME BADGE

CLEAN UNIFORM

SHOES SHINED

WHEN serving customers on the driveway, Conoco Service Station salesmen should wear: (1) A smile. (2) A shave. (3) A CLEAN uniform. (4) A Conoco cap as part of the uniform. (5) Shoes that are shined. (6) Hair trimmed and combed. (7) A Conoco name badge

Guidelines for attendants from 1936 *Service Manual*.

Location unknown (1936).

Attendant giving direction with
Touraide (1936).

Corpus Christi, Texas (circa 1934).

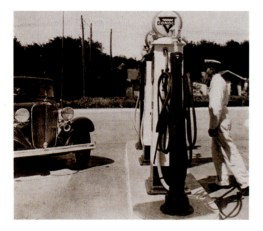

Location unknown (1936).

Panel delivery truck (note round porcelain door sign,
circa 1934).

1937 Rodeo team, Hobbs, New Mexico (notice fleet
of tank trucks in background).

Corpus Christi, Texas (circa 1934).

Maryville, Missouri (circa 1950).

Marshall, Missouri (circa 1950).

Somewhere in Missouri (circa 1950).

"Team" of service attendants waiting on a customer.

Somewhere in Missouri (circa 1950).

Sidewalk display.

Topeka, Kansas (1954).

Window display.

Dallas, Texas (1954).

Denver, Colorado (1954).

Location unknown (notice script top pumps and oil racks, 1953).

18-quart capacity metal oil rack with porcelain sign (42.5" tall). $350-450

1951 Martin and Schwartz Model 80 gas pump with fiberglass script top. $600-1200

Location unknown (note script top pumps and curbside sign, 1953).

Hutchinson, Kansas (1954).

Denver, Colorado (1954).

Fort Worth, Texas (1954).

Broadmoor Hotel, Colorado Springs, Colorado (1959).

Oklahoma City, Oklahoma (1954).

Location unknown (1953).

Sales tips from the May-June 1954 edition of *The Red Triangle Magazine*.

Pump islands and driveways are your station's "front door." Shine 'em up

Neat, orderly displays in your salesroom add customers and build business

Customers notice *you* and your salesmen, too! Can you pass inspection?

Location unknown (1953).

Houston, Texas (1953).

Location unknown (note script top Martin & Schwartz Model 80 pumps, 1955).

Gainesville, Texas (1954).

Cheyenne, Wyoming (1960)

New Conoco truck design (circa 1929).

Charles Lindbergh refueling the "Spirit of St. Louis," Salt Lake City, Utah (1927).

After the laboratory engines had picked what seemed to be the best formula, the new blend was put into Continental's fleet of trucks and cars at Ponca City, Denver, Butte, Pueblo, and Salt Lake City, to find out how it would perform in actual service in all kinds of road and weather conditions.

Refinery Truck Fleet (circa 1941).

CHAPTER TWO

MOTOR OILS

Conoco and Marland both began producing passenger car motor oils as early as 1921. It was Marland, however, who held the patent for the first canned passenger oil product from the new Continental Oil Company founded in 1929. This product was "Germ Processed" motor oil.

Since the introduction of Germ Processed oil in 1929, there have been six major kinds of Conoco automobile motor oil produced through 1970: Motorine, Nth Motor Oil, HD Motor Oil, Super Motor Oil, Par Motor Oil, and Motorine HD. The following is a description of these oils, when they were introduced and dropped, and how they were packaged. I have omitted Super Motor Oil from the descriptive list because there were so many different variations.

PRODUCT	YEAR INTRODUCED	YEAR DROPPED
Germ Processed	1922	1940
Motorine	1936	Late '60s
Nth Motor Oil	1941	1954
HD	1941	1955
Super Motor Oil	1950	1987
Par Motor Oil	1957	1988
Motorine	1959	1972

These dates are as accurate as possible based on company literature and advertisements. Some products may have still been on the shelf for a few years after the listed drop date until all of the product was sold. Unless otherwise mentioned, all cans are metal. Can types listed within the following descriptions are in chronological order.

GERM PROCESSED MOTOR OIL

Germ processing was the first motor oil additive ever used by any oil manufacturer. Germ Processing was a special oiliness (polar) additive invented and patented by two British scientists, Wells and Southcombe, in 1918. It was made from castor oil components. In 1934, Conoco developed a synthetic version called GD-160, later called MDS. This MDS was the material referred to as "Oil Plating" on cans

Booklet describing Germ Processed Oil Plating (1937). $5-15

and in advertisements. Germ Processed was chosen as the name of the first motor oil because it was a "germ of an idea!"

Germ Processed motor oil was run in a "destruction test" on the Indianapolis track in December 1933. Six identical Chevrolet cars were run continuously at a rate of 50 mph. One car used Germ Processed oil and the other five used competitive oils. No oil addition was allowed during the test. The car using Conoco's Germ Processed motor oil went 4,729 miles before engine failure. That was 1,409.2 miles and 116.88% over the average and 42.5% farther than the nearest competitor. AAA gave the product its sanction number 3001 after this test. During 1933-1934, the AAA insignia was on Conoco's test cars.

In the early '30s, Conoco's Germ Process oil became available in refinery-sealed, one-quart cans. Prior to that, this product was only sold in bulk. There are nine different quart cans that were produced from 1930 to 1940. At a glance, all of the can types look the same. They have a white background with green trim. The following is a list of the nine different cans, discussing the distinguishing features of each one.

1. Words "Net ONE U.S. QUART Liquid" imprinted at the top of the can above the new Conoco triangle logo. A tilted block with the phrase "New and Improved" covers part of the "M" in Germ and the "S" and "E" in Processed. There is a plain green band under the "Motor Oil" caption.

2. Same design as above with the addition of the American Automobile Association insignia to the left of the logo. This emblem has "AAA" in green letters inside a red oval that states "Contest Board Certified Test" in white letters. At the top of the can, "Tested and Approved" is printed in green letters. Also printed near the bottom of the can, in green letters, is "Sanction #3001."

3. Same design as above with slogan "The Hidden Quart Stays Up In Your Motor and Never Drains Away" printed at the bottom of the can face.

4. Same design as above without the "NEW" block initiated with the first can.

5. The AAA emblem is dropped on this can and does not reappear anymore on any future cans. The contents statement moved near the bottom of the can, just above "The Hidden Quart Stays..." statement. Near the top of the can, where the contents statement had been located, one side is printed with slogan "First With Extra Film Strength" and the other side of the can has the slogan "First With Added Oiliness."

6. Same design as above but "The Hidden Quart Stays..." statement is replaced with "Oil Plates Your Engine."

7. Same design as above but the contents statement is moved to the very bottom of the can face, just under the "Oil Plates Your Engine" statement. This can is the most frequently found because it was used for the longest period of time.

8. Same design as above but the slogan "First With Added Oiliness" replaces the slogan "First With Extra Film Strength" and is now on both sides of the can.

9. Same design as above minus the "First With Added Oiliness" slogans.

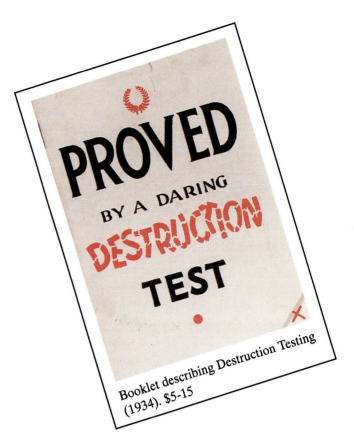

Booklet describing Destruction Testing (1934). $5-15

Type 1 Germ Processed 5-quart and 1-quart cans. $20-50

Type 4 Germ Processed 5-quart can.
$20-50

Type 7 Germ Processed 1-quart can.
$20-40

Type 9 Germ Processed 5-quart can. $20-50

Two Type 7 Germ Processed 5-quart
cans (note that one can is smooth and
the other has a ridge above the Conoco
logo). $20-50

Different 5-quart Germ Processed cans. $20-50

MOTORINE

Motorine Motor Oil was developed as a low-cost alternative to "Germ Processed" Motor Oil. This oil was 100% paraffin based. There are six known can styles.

1. This can has a plain white background. There is no triangle logo on the face of the can. The word "Motorine" is printed in large red letters in the center of the face of the can. Underneath this is a narrow green band with the slogan "A Fine Paraffin Base Motor Oil" in white letters across the green band. Under the green band is a red band with "Manufactured & Refinery Sealed By Continental Oil Company" in white letters. At the bottom of the face of the can is the contents statement in black letters with a white background. This can is fairly rare.
2. White can with double cross-hatch lines. The Conoco logo is outlined inside and out in the center of the can. Under the logo is a wide black band with "Motorine" in white letters. The slogan "A Fine Paraffin Base Motor Oil" appears on two lines across the bottom of the face.

3. Same design as previous can but with solid Conoco logo (circa 1948).
4. Same design with phrase "For Service "ML-MM" under green band.
5. Similar to previous cans but made of a composite material. There is no Conoco logo and the slogan "A Fine Paraffin Base" is also dropped from this can.
6. Same design as above but in a plastic can with a change in the lettering style.

Type 1 Motorine 5-quart and 1-quart cans. $20-40

Type 3 Motorine 1-quart can. $15-30

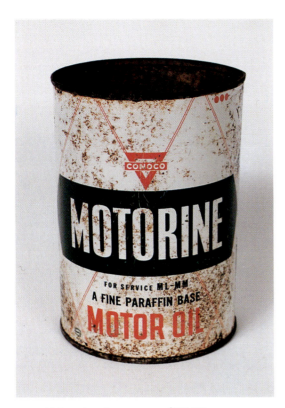

Type 4 Motorine 1-quart can. $15-30

Nth Motor Oil used an additive called Thialkene, a special oxidation inhibitor. Nth Motor Oil was used in the second "destruction test" which was run in Death Valley in 1940. Nth went 13,398.8 miles. This was 111.29% over the average and 73.67% better than the nearest competitor. One-quart "Nth" cans were made in four known styles.

1. White can with a green oval containing "Nth" in white letters. Under the oval, in small red letters, are the words "[Germ Processed]." There is a small Conoco logo near the bottom of the can outlined inside and out with fine green lines.
2. Wide, single cross-hatched line background with the Conoco logo outlined inside and out with red lines.
3. Same design as above but without the outline of the Conoco logo. (Conoco changed to this logo without the outline around 1948).
4. Double cross-hatched lines with solid Conoco logo.

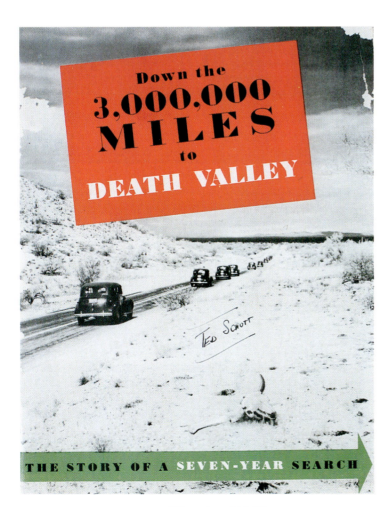

Book describing Nth Motor Oil testing. $10-20

Type 1 Nth 5-quart can. $20-50

Type 2 Nth 1-quart can. $15-30

Type 3 Nth 1-quart can. $15-30

HD MOTOR OIL

HD was Conoco's first detergent motor oil. Engines in those days were usually heavily sludged and the introduction of a detergent oil in a really dirty engine was sometimes hazardous. This fear still remains today in the fact that some people are reluctant to change brands of oil in their engines. There was one known can style.

1. White can with single cross-hatched lines. Conoco logo appears in red near the bottom of the can face. Above the logo is the statement "For Service DG-MS" in small print. Majority of the can face contains text "Conoco H-D Motor Oil".

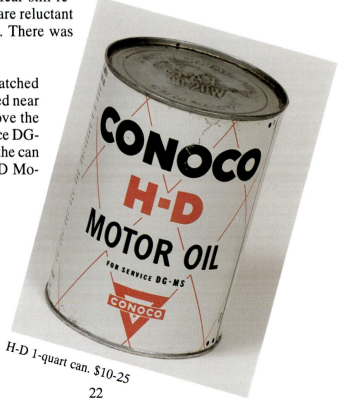

H-D 1-quart can. $10-25

SUPER MOTOR OIL

There is not a breakdown of Super cans due to the large number of varieties produced. Pictured are some examples.

Various Super 1-quart cans (top two are composite). $10-25

PAR MOTOR OIL

Par Motor Oil was a straight mineral oil developed as a low-priced product that could be used in old, badly worn cars with heavy oil consumption. There are three known can styles.

1. White cross-hatched background with colored band around bottom of the can containing words "PAR MOTOR OIL."[2]
2. Solid gray can with red "target" in center of can containing "Par Motor Oil."
3. Green and white can with two silver stripes separating the green area from white area.

Type 2 Par 1-quart can. $10-25

Various Super 4-quart and one 5-quart can. $15-35

23

Motorine HD was a heavy duty motor oil developed for late model passenger cars, gasoline powered trucks, and high speed automotive diesel engines. Motorine HD contained effective detergents to reduce ring sticking, engine deposits, and valve lifter troubles. There are three known can styles.

1. White, single cross-hatched background with a red band around the bottom of the can containing the words "Motorine HD Motor Oil".
2. Solid red can with a white "target" in the center with the words "Motorine HD Motor Oil".
3. Same as above but with a composite can.

I do not pretend to believe that this list is absolutely complete. However, to the best of my knowledge it is accurate for all one quart motor oil cans produced from the late 1920s through around 1970. As shown in the photographs, there were also five-quart and four-quart containers produced in many of these products and styles.

Type 1 Motorine HD 1-quart can. $10-25

Type 2 Motorine HD 1-quart can. $10-25

Tracon Supreme and Diesel motor oil 1-quart cans. $10-25

Products other than oil and gasoline have played an important marketing role for many oil companies through the years. Conoco was not an exception. Since its humble beginning in 1875, Conoco has marketed many diverse products through its stations and bulk plants. These products include, but are not limited to, greases, lubes, antifreeze, automatic transmission fluid, household oils, lighter fluid, oil filters, batteries, gasoline additives, and waxes.

Of these odd products, one item seems to stand out as a favorite of many collectors, including myself. The four-ounce can of household oil has become a very popular collectible. I believe this has occurred for several reasons. First of all, handy oilers (as they are referred to) are relatively inexpensive compared to some collectibles. Secondly, almost all oil companies marketed a can of household oil at one time or another. This makes it possible for a collector to specialize in one type of collectible rather than one company's collectibles.

The following pages identify a few of the various products I have been able to uncover. I have seen evidence, however, that there are hundreds more non-motor oil products bearing the Conoco name that are worthy collectibles.

Plastic Handy Oil tube (1950s). $5-15

4-oz. Household Oil can (Late 1950s). $10-25

4-oz. Household Oil can (1954). $10-25

1-quart container of F-Z Spring Lubricant (1930s). $20-45

1-gallon container of Anti-Squeak Oil (1930s). $20-45

4-oz. Lighter Fluid can (1960s). $10-25

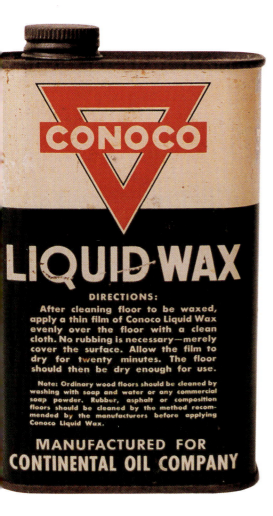

1-pint container of Liquid (floor) Wax (1930s). $20-45

Back of Liquid Wax can (note colorful ad for Touraide).

1-gallon container of Anti-Squeak Oil (1950s). $20-40

10-lb. container of Racelube and Medium Pressure Lubricant (1930s). $15-40

1-lb. container of Light Pressure Lubricant and No.2 Cup Grease (1930s). $10-25

1-lb. container of Pumplube No.1 and Medium Pressure Lubricant (1950s). $10-25

10-lb. container of Racelube and Super Lube Grease (1950s).
$15-40

1-lb. container of Racelube Grease (1950s).
$10-25

25-lb. container of Universal Gear Lubricant (1950s). $20-35

1-lb. container of Super Lube Grease (1960s). $10-25

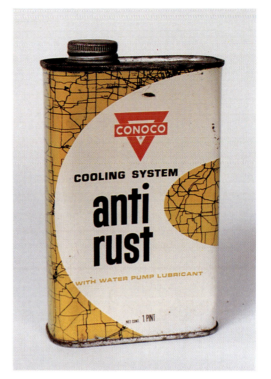

1-pint container of Anti Rust with graphic map background (1960s). $15-35

1-gallon container of Antifreeze (1950s). $15-35

1-quart container of Scat Two Cycle Oil
(1960s). $10-25

12-oz. container of Hydraulic
Brake Fluid (1950s). $10-20

1-pint container of Car Cleaner-Polish
(1960s). $10-20

4-oz. and 8-oz. Tunes It cans with graphic map background
(1960). $10-15

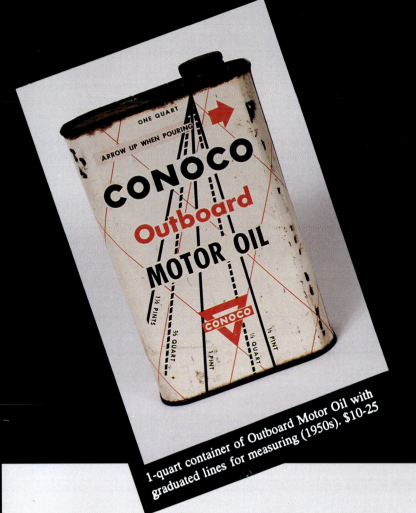

1-quart container of Outboard Motor Oil with graduated lines for measuring (1950s). $10-25

1-quart container of Outboard Motor Oil
(1950s). $10-25

8-oz. container of Outboard Motor Oil
(1960s). $10-20

1-quart plastic container of
Outboard Motor Oil (1960s).
$10-20

CHAPTER FOUR
ROADMAPS AND THE TOURAIDE TRAVEL SERVICE

Like almost every other oil company operating in the United States during the 1900s, Conoco provided its patrons with complimentary road maps to assist them while travelling. The first known road maps were distributed by Gulf in 1914, and Conoco began distributing them in 1920. The early Conoco road maps were somewhat different than the fold-out maps used today. From 1920 to around 1926, they were made of a cardboard-like paper with the map folded and glued inside the covers.

Starting around 1927, Conoco switched to the fold-out style. For most collectors, the maps dating from 1927 to 1931 are some of the most desirable. The maps produced during this time period are very colorful and filled with illustrations.

Beginning with the 1928 maps, I have identified fourteen different types of state road maps issued through 1970. The following is a description of the different map covers for identification purposes:

1928: Graphic cover
1929: Graphic with date on front cover
1930: Graphic with date on front cover
1931: Graphic with date on front cover
1932: Compass on front cover
1933: Pink with mermaids and fish on front cover
1934-35: North America continent on cover with slogan "Every Conoco Station is A Branch of The" printed across Mexico
1936-45: North America continent on cover with above text printed below the bottom of the continent
1946: Same as above with "For Long Trips Ask Your Conoco Mileage Merchant About Touraide" text instead of above text
1947-48: Cartoon family on cover with Conoco triangle logo outlined in green
1949-59: Same as above without the outlined logo
1960-63: Striped cover with hat and hand
1964-66: Color scenic photo with logo and state name at top of map
1967-?: Same as above but with slogan "Touraide Map Of" preceding the state name

This list is not all-inclusive of the maps produced and distributed during this era. There were many U.S., regional U.S., and city maps that were distributed also.

One obstacle that I recently overcame (with the help of a map dealer) is the ability to accurately date maps from the years where the date was not printed on the cover or over the period of years when all of the covers were the same (i.e. 1936 to 1945). During this period of time in the United States, there were two primary map manufacturers, Rand McNally and Gousha. Each of these companies used a different coding system to identify the specific year each map was produced. During this period, however, almost all Conoco maps were made by Gousha.

INDEX OF MAP CODES

YEAR	Rand MacNally	Gousha	YEAR	Rand MacNally	Gousha
1919	A	-	1949	9	W
1920	B	-	1950	0	X
1921	C	-	1951	1	Y
1922	D	-	1952	2	Z
1923	E	-	1953	3	AA
1924	F	-	1954	4	BB
1925	G	-	1955	5	CC
1926	H	-	1956	6	DD
1927	I	A	1957	7	EE
1928	J	B	1958	8	FF
1929	K	C	1959	9	GG
1930	L	D	1960	0	HH
1931	M	E	1961	1	II
1932	N	F	1962	2	JJ
1933	O	G	1963	3	KK
1934	P	H	1964	4	LL
1935	Q	I	1965	5	MM
1936	R	J	1966	6	NN
1937	S	K	1967	7	OO
1938	T	L	1968	8	PP
1939	U	M	1969	9	QQ
1940	V	N	1970	0	RR
1941	W	O	1971	1	SS
1942	X	P	1972	2	TT
1943	Y	Q	1973	3	UU
1944	Z	R	1974	4	VV
1945	5	S	1975	5	WW
1946	6	T	1976	6	XX
1947	7	U	1977	7	YY
1948	8	V	1978	8	ZZ

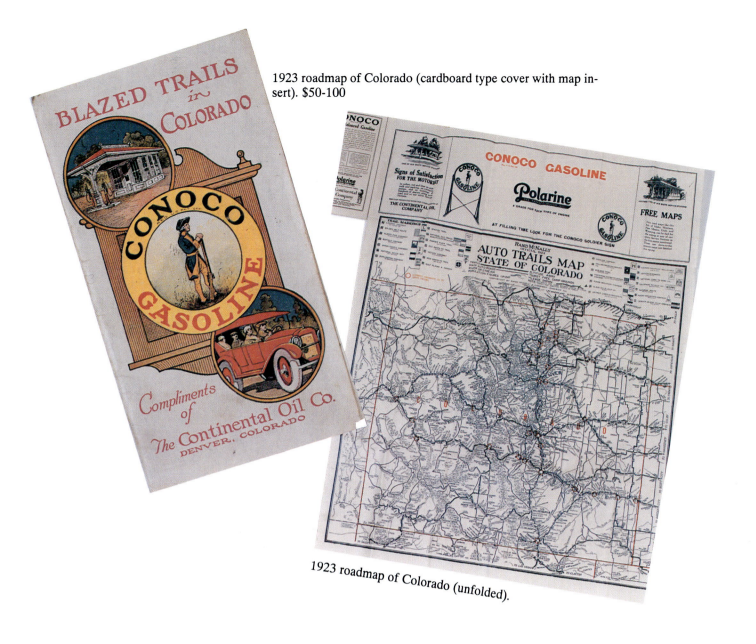

1923 roadmap of Colorado (cardboard type cover with map insert). $50-100

1923 roadmap of Colorado (unfolded).

For example, let's look at a map from the period with the most common cover design (1949-59). At the bottom of each individual map is a series of numbers and letters. The easiest place to locate this code is on the smaller city maps located on the flipside of the main map. Shown on page 45 is a close-up of the city of Savannah, Georgia. The code is 6-CC-630-C. If you look under the Gousha code "CC", we discover that this is a 1955 Georgia map. This seems to be a very accurate system of dating these maps. It may seem awkward at first because the code is printed in such small letters, but it gets easier with practice.

In 1930, Conoco took the road map service a step further, opening the Conoco Travel Bureau in Denver, Colorado. This department was responsible for distribution of road maps and the unique Touraide trip planning service. It was this Touraide service that set Conoco apart from most of the competition.

From 1930 through 1935, this service included a customized packet of road maps and hotel, camping, and state attractions guides. The Touraide service would outline the customer's trip route using the best available roads. Starting in 1936, all of the maps and guides were bound together in one book and sent to the customer. This book was called the Touraide. In addition to maps and hotel and camping guides, the Touraide also included price rates for lodging and identified Conoco stations along the route. This program was very similar to the services that the American Automobile Association (AAA) offers, except it was free.

This program immediately became extremely popular, and by 1934 over 1.1 million trips had been planned by the Conoco Travel Bureau. The program continued in this format until 1958, when it was replaced with a road atlas service. In the late 1960s it was phased out completely, due to high operating costs. An indicator of this cost was evident in 1960, when Conoco dealers started charging patrons 25¢ for the travel guides. Many travellers were dependent on this service and looked to Conoco stations as clean, friendly places to stop along their route. Customers as well as employees were sad to see this unique service end.

In addition to the Touraide book or maps, the Conoco Travel Bureau also provided customers of the early and mid-1930s with a Conoco Passport, mail forwarding stickers, and window identification decals. The Passport was a small booklet provided to customers for recording trip expenses and vehicle service records. The mail forwarding stickers were supplied for customers to have their mail forwarded to them in care of Conoco stations along their pre-planned trip route.

I am aware of at least eight different styles of Touraide books.

1936-45: Tan cover with green Touraide lettering. At least one exception to this cover during this time period is the 1939-40 editions which commemorated the Golden Gate Exposition in San Francisco.

1946-49: Red cover with cars coming down a winding mountain road.

1950-52: Photograph cover with a woman in red shirt sitting next to a lake.

1953-58: Cartoon cover of a family in a convertible driving through a mountain pass.

1959: Photograph cover with a man standing at a scenic overlook.

1960-65: Photograph cover of a man and woman sitting next to a mountain lake. 25¢ price on cover.

1966: Interstate Travel Guide.

1928 roadmap of Utah (Fold-out type). $40-75

Inside tri-fold of 1928 map.

1929 roadmap of Colorado (great graphics). $40-75

Inside tri-fold of 1929 map.

Inside half of 1929 map.

1930 roadmap of Nebraska (most graphic Conoco map). $30-65

Inside half of 1930 map.

Inside tri-fold of 1930 map.

1931 ROAD MAP OF
WYOMING

FILL UP WITH
ONOCO PRODUCTS

the joys of trouble-free
al... the satisfaction of
omy and safety gained
ugh the use of Conoco
cts.

OCO BALANCED BLEND
OLINE combines the three
ents which give the perfect
ice of power, mileage,
starting, acceleration and
om from knocking.

OCO ETHYL GASOLINE...
o Balanced Blend Gasoline
Ethyl Anti-Knock Fluid...
ates knocks, makes motors
oler, lengthens motor life.

OCO GERM-PROCESSED
R OIL reduces motor wear,
s starting easier, lowers
ne and oil consumption
e of its added oiliness and
ative lubricity.

with Conoco products at the
f the Conoco Red Triangle.

TRAVEL THE
CONOCO WAY

The CONOCO TRAVEL BUREAU offers a no-cost service to motorists in the detailed planning of tours to any section. The Bureau supplies marked maps of best routes, information on hotels, camps, resorts, sports and points of interest . . . supplies you with a CONOCO PASSPORT which is your key to an individualized service from any of the thousands of Red Triangle stations in Conocoland—Scenic America. Write for free descriptive booklet, addressing Conoco Travel Bureau, Denver, Colorado.

CONOCO COUPON BOOKS are handy, convenient, practical, on long or short trips. They obviate the necessity of carrying large amounts of cash; eliminate waits for change. They provide a precise record of car operating expense. Conoco Coupon Books on Sale at all Conoco Stations.

1931 roadmap of Wyoming. $25-50

noco Germ Processed
tor Oil penetrates and
bines with the metal
aces of your motor.

"HIDDEN QUART
stays up in your
or and never drains
y" provides an un-
lled degree of safety
lessens motor wear.

Travel
ARIZONA
with

**Every Conoco Station
is a branch of the**

CONOCO
TRAVEL
BUREAU

Wherever and whenever you buy Conoco Balanced Blend gasoline or Conoco Ethyl gasoline you will notice their quick-starting, sustained power, and long mileage results, because they are Blended for Season and Section.

1932 roadmap of Arizona. $15-30

CONOCO TRAVEL BUREAU

Inside tri-fold of 1932 map (shows details about Conoco Travel Bureau).

1933 roadmap of Nebraska (notice mermaids and fish on front cover). $15-30

1947-1948 roadmap style (1948 North Carolina/South Carolina). $10-20

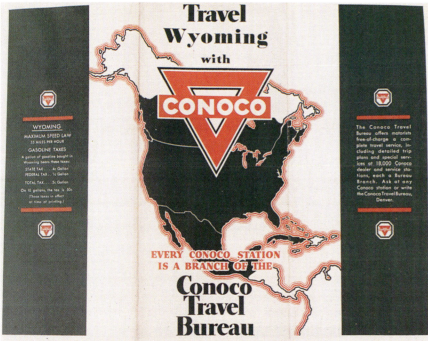

1934-1935 roadmap style (1934 Wyoming). $15-30

1949-1959 roadmap style (1955 Georgia). $10-20

1936-1945 roadmap style (1936 Colorado). $15-30

1946 roadmap of Washington. $15-30

1960-1963 roadmap style (1961 Kansas). $10-20

1964-1966 roadmap style (1965 Illinois). $5-10

1936 United States Map and Mileage Chart. $10-20

Inside tri-fold of 1936 U.S. map (note detail description of Touraide Service).

1967-? roadmap style (1967 Arizona). $5-10

Different 1936 United States Map and Mileage Chart. $10-20

1939 United States Map and Mileage Chart. $10-20

Inside tri-fold of 1936 U.S. map (note detailed description of Conoco Travel Bureau).

Inside tri-fold 1939 U.S. map.

Mid 1960s Marketing Manager's map case (53 dividers with city, state, regional, and national maps). $150-250

1945 United States Map and Mileage Chart. $10-20

Brochure explaining Travel Bureau and Passport Service (1932). $5-15

Gousha coding on 1955 Georgia map of Savannah (code 6-CC-630-C).

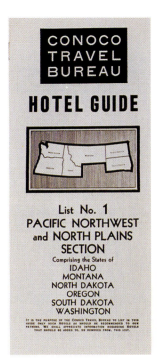

Early 1930s Hotel Guides. $5-10

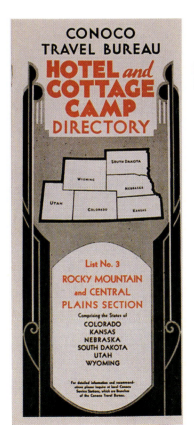

Rocky Mountains Hotel and Cottage Camp Directory (1936). $5-10

Early 1930s Cottage Camp Directory. $5-10

1933-1934 state travel guides for Wyoming, Colorado, and Utah.
$5-10

1934 Guides to Yellowstone and the Ozark Mountains. $5-10

Late 1930s Hotel Directories. $5-10

1933-1934 state travel guides for Missouri, Indiana, Georgia & Florida, and The Virginias. $5-10

(L-R) 1935, 1934, and 1936 Passports. $15-30

Postage forwarding stickers and stamp envelope (early 1930s). $5-10

Travel Club window stickers (early 1930s). $5-15

1936-1945 Edition Touraide (1936). $10-25

Detailed trip route from 1936 Touraide.

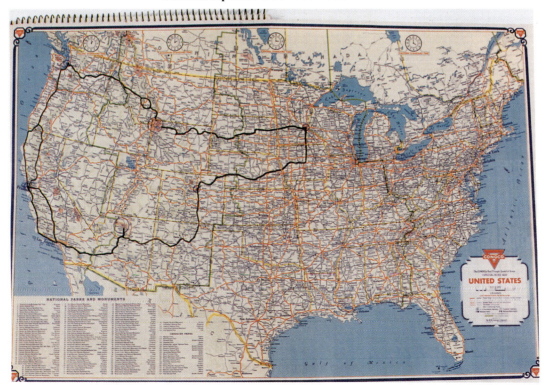

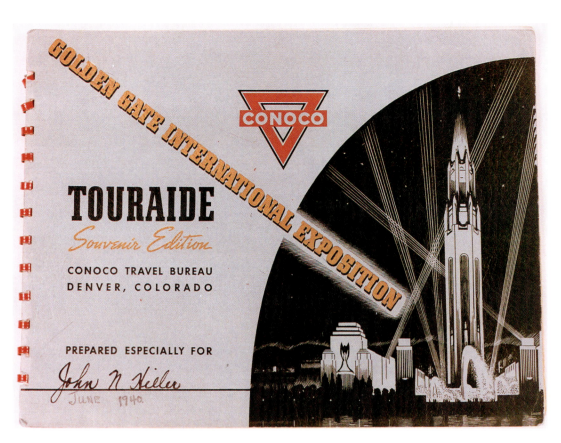

1939 Golden Gate Expo Edition of Touraide. $10-25

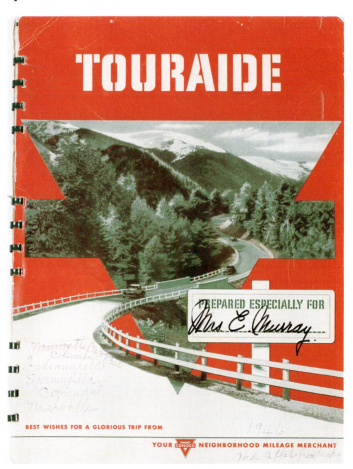

1946-1949 Edition Touraide (1946). $10-25

1950-1952 Edition Touraide (1950). $10-20

Postcards from inside
back pocket of 1950
Touraide. $5

TOURAIDE

1959 Edition Touraide (1st atlas type without trip planning service). $10-20

TOURAIDE
Prepared Especially for
1953

Best Wishes for a Grand Trip from

YOUR MILEAGE MERCHANT

1953-1958 Edition Touraide (1953). $10-20

Pocket
TOURAIDE
TRAVEL GUIDE

1963 Pocket Touraide. $5-10

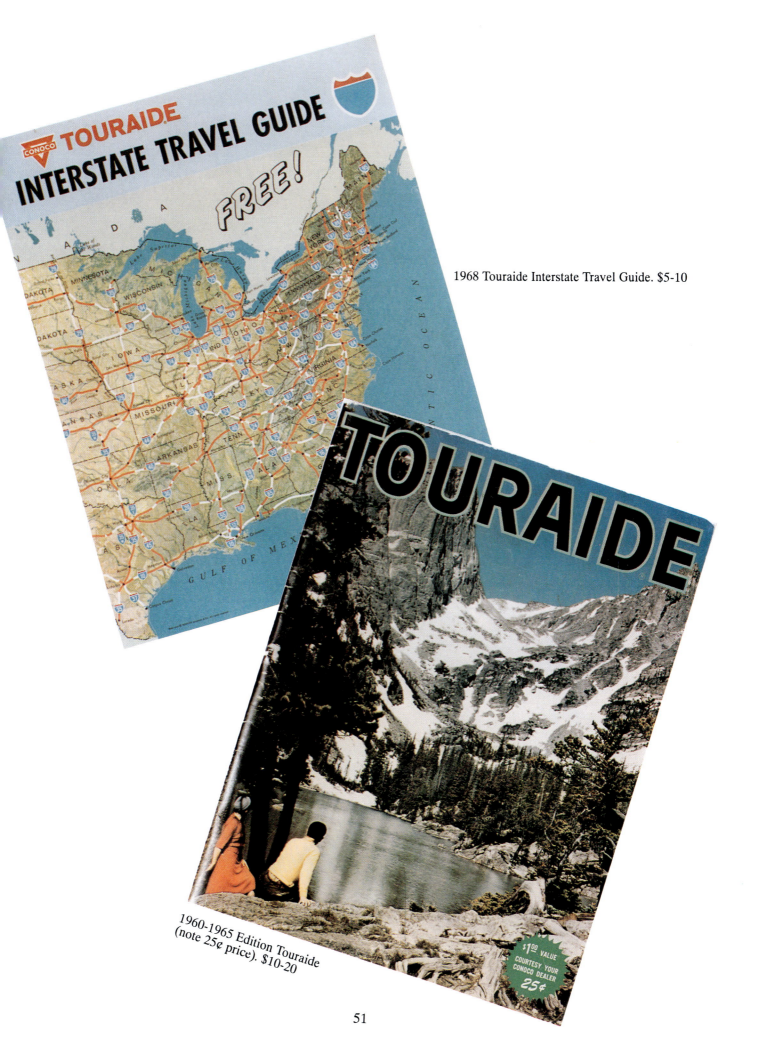

1968 Touraide Interstate Travel Guide. $5-10

1960-1965 Edition Touraide
(note 25¢ price). $10-20

Onc of thc grcat things about sign collccting is the fact that there are so many different signs available. These signs were used for pumps, oil racks, windows, display racks, rest room doors, and were placed outside stations as advertisement. Most of the signs used during this period were porcelain. It is becoming much more difficult, however, to find non-porcelain metal signs still in good condition. The porcelain signs are much more durable and were able to withstand the weather and rough handling over the years.

The most common signs I have found while collecting are the porcelain pump plates used during the 1940s through the 1960s. These signs are all triangular shaped and come in five different varieties. The styles are as follows:

1. Red and white sign with "Conoco" printed across center. Used for both gasoline pumps and oil racks. This sign is approximately 8" wide.
2. Green and white sign with "Conoco" printed across center. Used for pumps only. This sign is slightly larger than the above sign (slightly less than 9" wide).
3. Red and white sign with "Royal" printed across center. Also used for pumps only. Same size as above No. 2.
4. Red and white sign with "Super" printed across center. Same use and size as Nos. 2 and 3.
5. Black and white sign with "Diesel" printed across center. Same use and size as Nos. 2, 3, and 4.

The "Super" and "Diesel" versions are very rare. The other three types of pump plates are relatively common. From my research, I have discovered that the No. 1 sign type was used initially on pumps and then on oil racks. No. 2 and No. 3 replaced the No. 1 type as a pump sign.

Another fairly common sign which would make a good addition to any collection is the die-cut triangle sign used outside stations for advertisement. This sign is approximately 40" tall and 44" wide. The sign in my collection (pictured on page 54) is outlined in green. As I discussed in the earlier chapters pertaining to maps and cans, this green outline is useful in

Type 1 porcelain pump plate and oil rack sign (approx. 8" x 7.5"). $50-100

dating Conoco memorabilia. Conoco stopped using this green outline on its logos around 1948. After 1948, all of the triangle logos were solid.

Gasoline globes date back to the early 1900s when vendors used the lighted globes to attract customers at night. Once again, Conoco was not an exception. Globe collecting could present a problem for many novice collectors. This is primarily due to the expense and knowledge required to collect globes. The most common Conoco globes from the 1950s and 1960s are selling for around $150. From there, prices climb steadily based on rarity and age. Some globes can easily sell for $2000 to $3000.

The other problem with globe collecting is the fact that there are currently several hundred kinds of reproduction globes on the market. Potential globe buyers should be wary of the reproduction market and do their homework before buying. Two collectors, Scott Benjamin and Wayne Henderson, have written a very detailed guide to gas globe collecting. I highly recommend using this guide or something similar before jumping head first into globe collecting.

Type 2 porcelain pump plate (9.5" x 8.5").
$50-100

Type 3 porcelain pump plate (9.5" x 8.5"). $50-100

Types 1, 2, and 3 pump plates. $50-100

Double-sided porcelain triangle (1930s-1040s, 44.25" x 39.25"). $250-400

Double-sided porcelain triangle (1950s, 6' 4" x 5' 11"). $150-250

Glass globe with red plastic body (1950s-1960s, 13.5" diameter). $150-250

Single-sided porcelain Marland Greasing Service (1920s, 40" x 28"). $150-300

Single-sided porcelain Conoco Greasing Service (1920s-1930s, 40" x 28"). $150-300

Single-sided porcelain truck door sign (1930s-1940s, 11" diameter). $350-500

Single-sided tin Germ Processed sign (1920s-1930s, 39.25" x 27.5"). $50-150

Double-sided porcelain Ethyl sign (1920s-1930s, 30" diameter). $150-300

Double-sided porcelain Super Motor Oil swinging sign (1950s, 27" x 30"). $250-400

Double-sided tin Nth curbside sign with embossed Conoco base (1940s, 31" x 36"). $150-250

Single-sided tin Super Motor Oil rack sign (1950s, 16.75" x 6").
$20-40

Single-sided porcelain Super pump sign (1950s, 12" x 5.25").
$30-50

Single-sided metal rest room signs (1950s-1960s, 10" x 5").
$150-250

Double-sided metal rest room signs with mounting flanges
(1950s-1960s, 10" x 5"). $150-250

Double-sided metal Batteries rack sign (1960s, 24.5" x 7.5").
$25-50

Double-sided metal credit cards sign (1950s-1960s, 24" x 18").
$50-100

SERVICE PRICES

CHARGE IT ON YOUR CONOCO CARD

TIRE REPAIR-TUBELESS	$1.00
TIRE REPAIR-TUBE TYPE	$1.50
ADJUST BRAKES	$2.50 ea
PACK U-JOINTS	$3.00
PACK FRONT WHEELS	$3.49 ea
FLUSH RADIATOR	$1.19
MOTOR TUNE-UP	$6.95 up
INSTALL ANTI-FREEZE	$2.98
WAX & POLISH	$8.90 up
SPECIAL TODAY	
RECHARGE BATTERY	$.98

Service menu board (1960s, 19" x 29.25"). $100-200

Double-sided metal pump price topper (1960s-1970s). $50-100

Window decal (1960s). $5-15

Window decal (1960s). $5-15

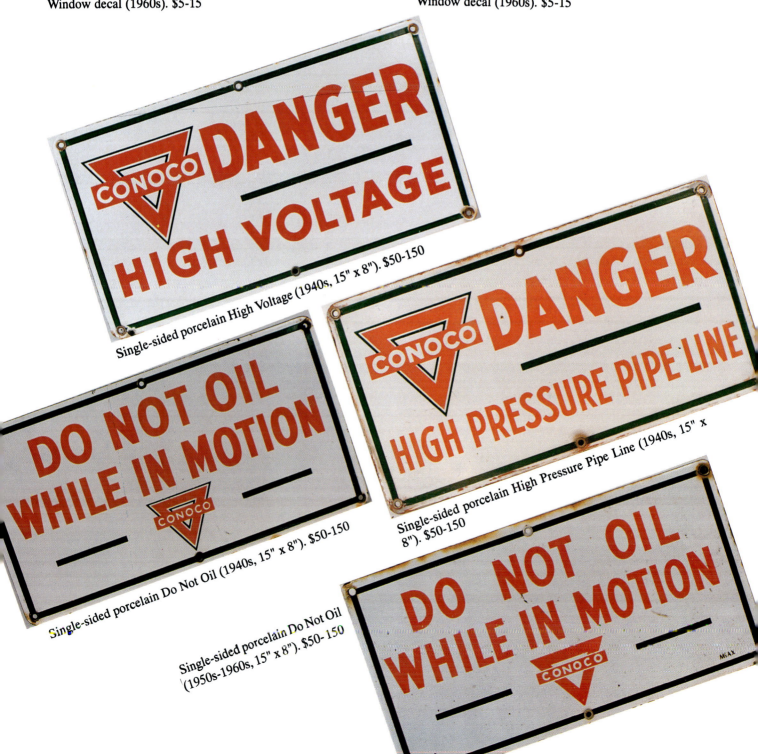

Single-sided porcelain High Voltage (1940s, 15" x 8"). $50-150

Single-sided porcelain Do Not Oil (1940s, 15" x 8"). $50-150

Single-sided porcelain High Pressure Pipe Line (1940s, 15" x 8"). $50-150

Single-sided porcelain Do Not Oil (1950s-1960s, 15" x 8"). $50-150

CAUTION
THIS WELL TIME CLOCK CONTROLLED
AND OPERATES INTERMITTENTLY
OPEN DISCONNECT SWITCH BEFORE
WORKING ON UNIT
CONTINENTAL OIL CO.

Single-sided porcelain Time Clock (1940s-1960s, 25.75" x 10").
$50-150

CAUTION
THIS WELL TIME-CLOCK CONTROLLED
AND OPERATES INTERMITTENTLY.
OPEN DISCONNECT SWITCH BEFORE
WORKING ON UNIT.
CONTINENTAL OIL COMPANY

Single-sided porcelain Time Clock (1940s-1960s, 15" x 8"). $50-
150

Single-sided porcelain well sign (1950s-1960s, 25.75" x 10").
$50-150

Single-sided porcelain well sign (1950s-1960s, 25.75" x 10").
$50-150

Single-sided porcelain lease sign (1940s-1960s, 30" x 20"). $75-150

Single-sided porcelain wall sign (1930s, 10' x 11"). $150-300

CHAPTER SIX
GIVEAWAYS AND PROMOTIONAL PROGRAMS

Giveaway and promotional program collectibles are possibly the easiest and most affordable way to start a collection. There are countless varieties of items available. Some good examples of giveaways are pens, pencils, key chains, matches, etc.

There is one promotional program in particular that I feel deserves recognition. This is the "Lucky Triangle" Program which began in the late 1950s and ended in the early 1960s. This program was introduced to promote the sale of Conoco canned motor oil products. A plastic "Lucky Triangle" was placed in the bottom of certain one-quart cans. These triangles could be collected by dealers or customers and redeemed like savings stamps for products from a catalog.

I have only seen examples of the red "Lucky Triangles" (like the ones pictured below). I have been told, however, that there were also some green ones which were worth more points than the red when redeemed.

Here is a collage of some of the items I have been able to find.

Figural gas pump salt & pepper shakers with box (1950s, 2.75" tall). $35-100

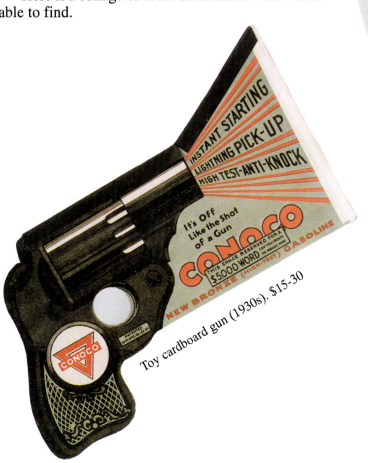

Toy cardboard gun (1930s). $15-30

Plastic Lucky Triangles (late 1950s or early 1960s). $10-25

Sleeve of golf balls and markers (1960s). $5-30

Paper kite (1960s). $30-50

Assorted cigarette lighters (1950s-1960s). $40-80

Winross metal toy truck (1960s, 8" long). $40-80

Various matchbook covers (1930s-1950s). $5

Deck of playing cards (1960s). $5-15

Various pens and mechanical pencils (1930s-1950s, note oil in top of two pens on far left). $10-35

Key chains (1930s-1940s). $10-30

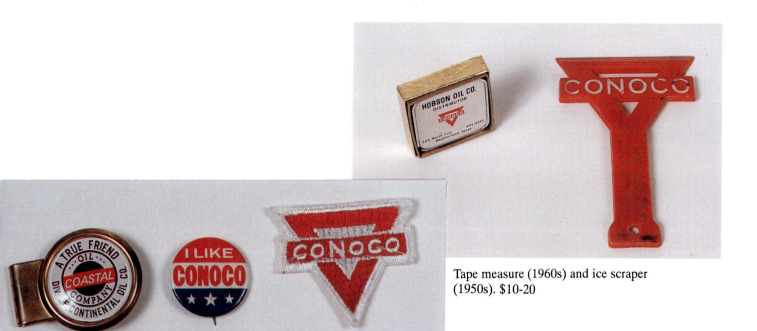

Tape measure (1960s) and ice scraper (1950s). $10-20

Money clip (1950s), "I Like Ike-like" pin (1950s), and cloth uniform patch (1950s-1960s). $5-40

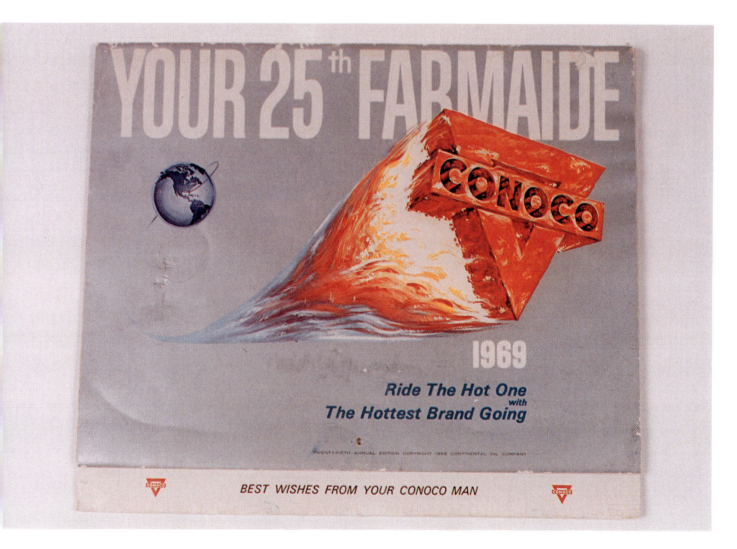

25th Edition Farmaide Calendar (1969). $10-25

Memo pad (1901, front). $15-40

Memo pad (1901, back).

Auto trash bag (1960s). $5-10

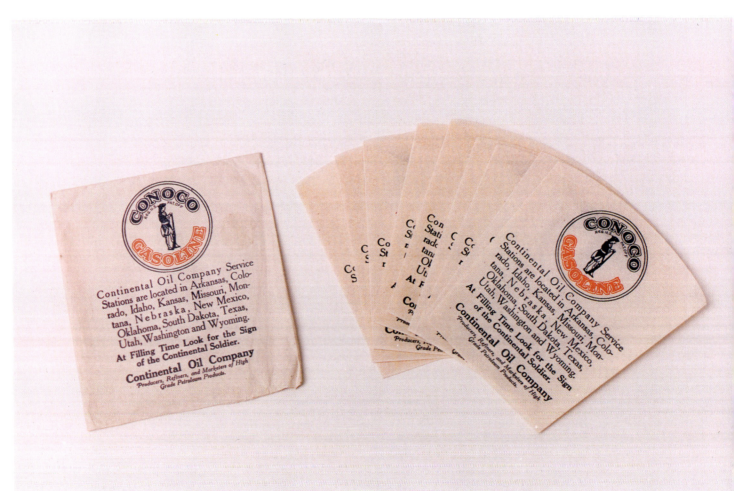

10 pack of paper drinking cups with envelope (1920s). $50-100

For some reason, banks have always been popular items for oil and gas marketing. Once again, Conoco was not an exception.

The most common vintage banks are probably the four-ounce oil can banks. These were distributed by Conoco from the 1930s to 1950s. These can banks were made in Germ Processed, Nth, and Super Motor Oil versions. My personal favorite and possibly the most unusual and sought-after is the "Fat Man" bank. These little guys were given away during the 1940s and 1950s. They are quite rare and are somewhat fragile because of their plastic composition. Both of these bank types are available from many other oil and gas companies as well.

In the mid-1980s, a new trend developed in oil and gas company bank collectibles. It was around then that the Ertl Company began making small truck banks with oil and gas company logos and colors. Since then, Spec-Cast and Scale Models have joined in to produce their own distinct banks. Several of these banks were issued in limited editions and have become quite collectible and have increased in value. For those of you new to this hobby, it important to the keep the box that comes with the bank. The market value of the bank is usually cut in half without the box.

"Fat Man" bank (1940s-1950s, 5" tall). $150-200

Ertl 1926 Mack Tanker (1989) No. 1 in series. $200-250

Nth and Super Motor Oil 4-oz. banks
(1940s-1950s, 3.5" tall). $30-45

Ertl Horses and Tankwagon (1990) No. 2 in series. $30-50

Ertl 1937 Ford Tanker (1991) No.3 in series. $30-40

Ertl International Tanker (1991) No. 4 in series. $25-40

Spec-Cast 1929 Model A Tanker (1992) No. 5 in series. $25-35

Ertl Diamond Reo Tractor Trailer (1992) No. 6 in series. $30-40

Ertl 1925 Kenworth Stake Truck (1993) No. 7 in series. $25-35

Spec-Cast 1932 Lockheed Vega (1993) No. 8 in series. $50-75

K-Line 1934 Riveted Tank Car (1994) No. 9 in series. $35-50

Scale Models 1929 International Marland (1992) No. 1 in series
(5000 produced). $35-50

Scale Models 1929 International Marland Sampler (1992) No. 1 in series (500 produced). $50-75

Scale Models 1920 International Marland (1992) No.2 in series (5000 produced). $35-50

Scale Models 1920 International Marland Sampler (1992) No. 2 in series (500 produced). $50-75

Scale Models 1927 Mack Marland (1993) No. 3 in series (5000 produced). $35-50

Scale Models 1927 Mack Marland Sampler (1993) No. 3 in series (500 produced). $50-75

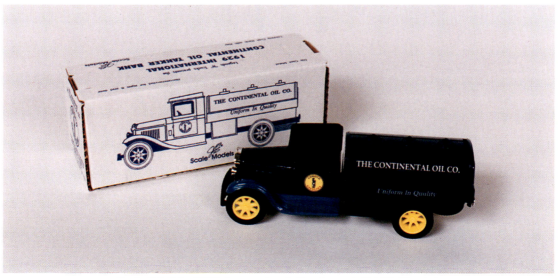

Scale Models 1929 International Continental (1992) No. 1 in series (5000 produced). $35-50

Scale Models 1929 International Continental Sampler (1992)
No. 1 in series (500 produced). $50-75

Scale Models 1920 International Continental (1993) No. 2 in
series (5000 produced). $35-50

Scale Models 1920 International Continental Sampler (1993)
No. 2 in series (500 produced). $50-75

Scale Models 1927 Mack Continental (1994) No. 3 in series (5000 produced). $35-50

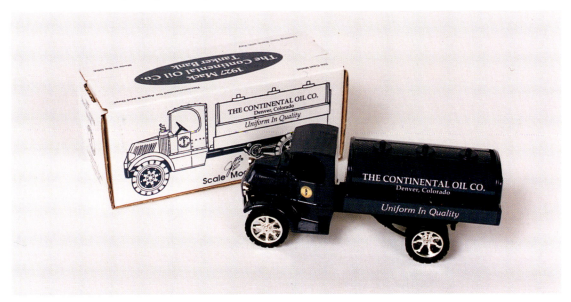

Scale Models 1927 Mack Continental Sampler (1994) No. 3 in series (500 produced). $50-75

Ertl Tanker (1990, not a bank, 20" long). $25-50

This chapter is reserved for items that do not really fit in the other chapters but are still excellent collectibles and deserve recognition.

Various tie bars/tacks and service pins (note 75th anniversary shovel-shaped tie bar). $25-75

Manager's desktop branding iron (1960s). $50-100

Wooden printer's blocks (.5" and 1"). $5-10

Western string tie (1960s). $25-50

Attendant's candy striped shirt and pants (1950s). $50-100

Lab coat worn during early 1960s road tests. $50-100

Various 1960s vintage plastic credit cards. $15-25

Credit slip holder (1960s). $15-25

Credit check cover (1950s). $10-20

Booklet of oil change stickers (1950s). $5-10

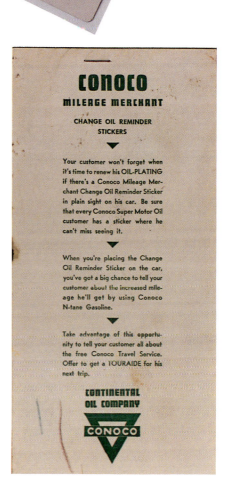

Credit card application
(1960s). $5-10

CONOCO HOME OIL CO.

WILLOW RIVER, MINN.   TEL. 10

DATE_____19_____

OCCUPATION_____   6051

SOLD TO_____

ADDRESS_____COUNTY

ORIGINAL

GASOLINE NOT SOLD FOR ILLUMINATING PURPOSES IN HOUSES.
WE SELL KEROSENE FOR LIGHTING AND HEATING PURPOSES ONLY WHEN
USED IN PROPER UTENSILS

KIND	GALLONS	PRICE	AMOUNT
CONOCO ETHYL			
CONOCO			
GERM PROCESS			
MOTORINE			
KEROSENE			
MINN. GAS TAX			

THIS IS TO CERTIFY THAT THE GASOLINE, KEROSENE OR FURNACE OIL COVERED BY
THIS SALE COMPLIES WITH THE SPECIFICATIONS OF THE MINNESOTA OIL INSPECTION
LAW, AND HAS BEEN INSPECTED AND APPROVED BY THE CHIEF OIL INSPECTOR.
                              CONOCO HOME OIL CO.

RECEIVED PAYMENT   CONOCO HOME OIL CO.

BY_____

GOODS RECEIVED

_____PURCHASER

_____SALESMAN

GOODS DELIVERED BY
                                        AGENT
                                        DRIVER

PRICES AND EXTENSION SUBJECT TO CORRECTION
THIS IS YOUR INVOICE — SAVE IT

McCASKEY, ALLIANCE, OHIO ☆

Bill slip for bulk product (1930s). $5

Back of 1929 envelope sent to a customer. $5-10

Post card (1960s). $5

Vehicle Expense Record Booklet (1940s). $5-10

Plastic map rack (1960s). $40-80

Windshield flyer (1960s). $5

Brass bulk oil ID tags. $5-15

Gas pump ad glass insert (1930s). $15-30

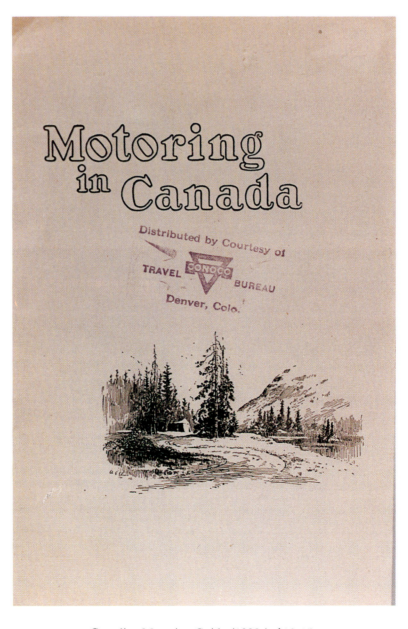

Canadian Motoring Guide (1930s). $10-15

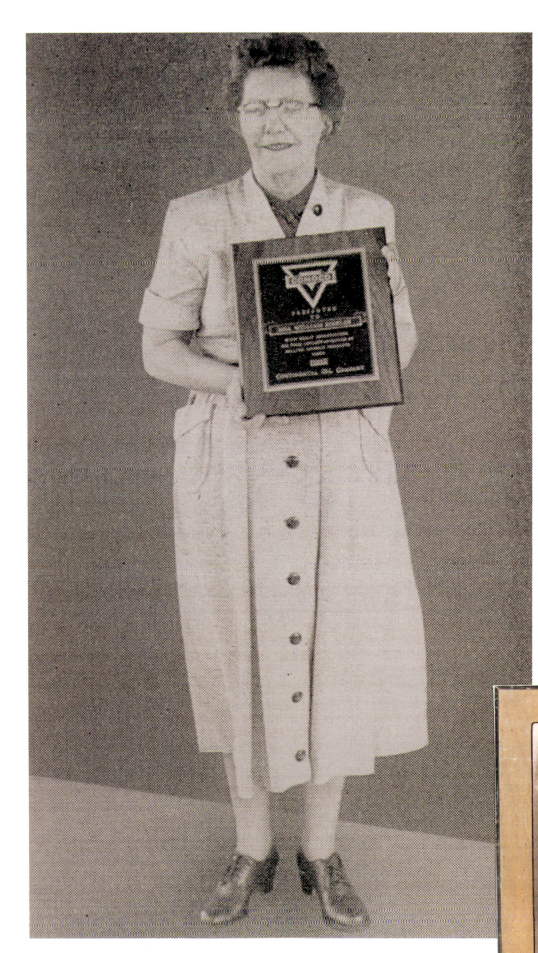

Copper service award. $40-80

Woman receiving copper service award.

Continental Oil Company stock certificate (100 shares). $5-10

Conoco Gas Journal (November 1918, front). $15-30

Conoco Gas Journal (November 1918, back).

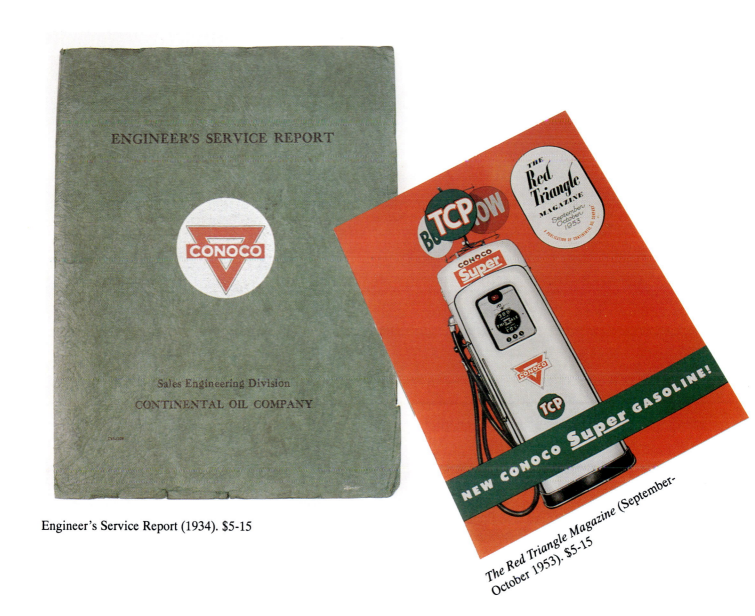

Engineer's Service Report (1934). $5-15

The Red Triangle Magazine (September-October 1953). $5-15

College recruiting booklet (1953). $10-15

Merchandising booklet (1933). $25-40

Service Manual (1936). $25-40

Super Motor Oil sales booklet (1950). $15-30

"Nutcracker" salesman's oil testing kit (1930s-1950s). $100-200

"Nutcracker" kit (inside).

Ad for "Rat Trap" salesman's grease testing kit from 1930s company publication.

Ad for "Nutcracker" from 1930s company publication.

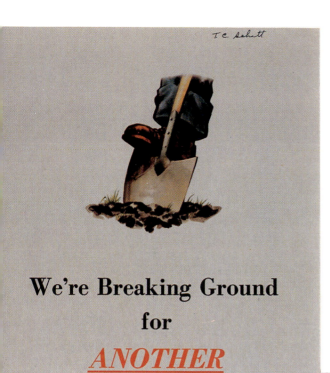

75th anniversary booklet (1950). $15-25

100th anniversary book (1975). $30-40

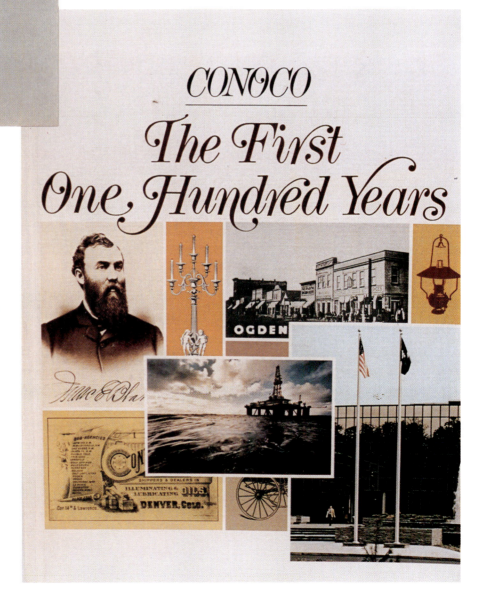

CHAPTER NINE
ADVERTISEMENTS

Perhaps no other form of nostalgia truly captures the essence of an era like advertisements. Ads accurately depict the people, cars, clothes, and terminology of an era.

In my research, I have uncovered many ads, both color and black and white, which appeared in popular publications, newspapers, and Conoco company magazines throughout the years. Some of these ads can still be found in various old issues of the *Saturday Evening Post*, *Life*, and many regional farm magazines.

On the following pages, I have included some of the more interesting ones that I have ran across. I hope you enjoy these windows into the past as much as I do.

Back cover of *The Red Triangle Magazine* (Christmas 1942).

Slicker Pickup !

This winter avoid grinding "dry-friction" starts.

Change now to Conoco N^{th} Motor Oil!

N^{th} Oil (patented) fastens *extra* lubricant to cylinder walls so closely it won't *all* drain down, even overnight! Always protects you . . . against corrosive combustion acids…from power-choking sludge and carbon due to wear. Make a date to OIL-PLATE today!

Your Conoco Mileage Merchant

CONOCO N^{th} MOTOR OIL

Back cover of *The Red Triangle Magazine* (January-February 1948).

The auto birth rate rises, *but there is still a fearful death rate!* . . .

You can whistle up your courage, trying to steer past the junkyard, or you can give your engine a change for its health . . . a change to protective internal OIL-PLATING, secured by changing to Conoco Nth motor oil—patented.

There is magnet-like action in Conoco Nth oil's added ingredient. Hence lubricant is attracted—OIL-PLATED!—direct to inner engine surfaces. The steadfast OIL-PLATING defies wear aplenty, and wear is the one big thing that increases sludge and carbon.

OIL-PLATING makes for all the mileage that your car has in it. So head for Conoco Nth motor oil now, at Your Mileage Merchant's Conoco station . . . *OIL-PLATE!* . . .

CONOCO

CONOCO
N$\underline{th}$
MOTOR OIL

don't let your car give up the ghost!

© 1946, Continental Oil Company

Saturday Evening Post (1946).

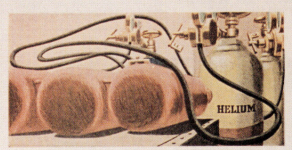

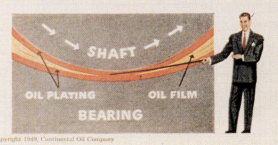

Saturday Evening Post (1949).

Weimaraners think they're People!

1. **Weimaraners** are the smartest dogs in the world. Product of 150 years of "selective breeding," these amazing gun-dogs display almost human intelligence. In the field, they do *instinctively* what most dogs take years to learn. One *Weimaraner* puts his master's other dogs into the kennel at night, closes the door and then goes into the house to sleep. "The only trouble with *Weimaraners*," say their owners, "is that they think they're people."

Color photograph courtesy TRUE, The Man's Magazine

2. **The Weimaraner** is the world's outstanding example of a dog bred to do a specific job better than it had ever been done before . . . just as the amazing new Conoco **Super** Motor Oil was "selectively designed" to *fight wear* in the engine of your car. Conoco **Super** OIL-PLATES your engine, to make it last longer, perform better, *use less gasoline and oil.*

3. **50,000 miles—no wear!** After a gruelling 50,000-mile road-test, engines lubricated with Conoco **Super** Motor Oil showed *no wear of any consequence* . . . an average of less than one one-thousandth inch on cylinders and crankshafts! Also proved: with proper crankcase drains and regular care, Conoco **Super** Motor Oil can give amazing economy. Average gasoline mileage for the last 5,000 was actually 99.77% as good as for the first 5,000.

CONTINENTAL OIL COMPANY, pioneer in oil-perfecting additives, and for over 25 years a leader in oil research, has more than 100 patents on discoveries that improve performance and lengthen the life of your car.

© 1950 **CONTINENTAL OIL COMPANY**

Saturday Evening Post (1950).

Centerfold of *The Red Triangle Magazine* (January-February 1953).

THE SATURDAY EVENING POST

A Nose for Pig Boats!

1. **Darting about like dolphins,** U. S. Navy submarines—
—equipped with modern versions of a fantastic Dutch invention
—recently "destroyed" almost an entire naval task force in
maneuvers off Newfoundland. Chief credit for this went to the
snorkel, a device which enables subs to breathe under water.
Invented by the Dutch, stolen by the Nazis and perfected by
the U. S. Navy, the snorkel has revolutionized naval warfare.

Saturday Evening Post (1950).

2. **Twice as fast under water** as pre-
war submarines—because it uses diesel engines instead of batteries—the snorkel-equip-
ped sub can stay submerged for weeks. The
snorkel is the latest word in naval protection
. . . just as new Conoco *Super* Motor Oil—
with OIL-PLATING—is the latest word in
protecting your engine against winter wear.

3. **50,000 Miles — No Wear!** After a punishing
50,000-mile road test, *with proper crankcase drains and regular care,* engines lubricated with new Conoco *Super* Motor
Oil showed *no wear of any consequence.* In fact, an average
of less than one one-thousandth inch on cylinders and crankshafts! This test also proved that Conoco *Super* Motor Oil
can give amazing economy. Gasoline mileage for the last
5,000 miles was actually 99.77% as good as for the first 5,000.

CONOCO
Super
MOTOR OIL

Now celebrating its 75th anniversary,
Continental Oil Company is still a pioneer
in oil-perfecting additives and a leader in
research, with more than 100 patents on
discoveries that improve performance and
lengthen the trouble-free life of your car.

©1950 **CONTINENTAL OIL COMPANY**

Are all Motor Oils Alike?

No—and your car can tell the difference!

If you use Conoco Super Motor Oil regularly, your car will show its appreciation by eating less—running better—living longer! Here's why:

- First of all, Conoco Super is manufactured from vacuum-distilled, solvent-refined, high V.I. paraffin base oils. That's mighty technical language but what it means to your car is that sludge and carbon are minimized.

- Conoco Super contains a patented Oil-Plating® ingredient which fastens a tough film of lubricant to moving engine parts. Oil stays attached to engine parts even when your car is not running. Thus you get easy starts in the morning, too.

- Conoco Super also contains a detergent—same principle as the modern synthetics. Dirt is *held* in suspension, drains out readily when the oil is changed.

- And the rust inhibitor in Conoco Super protects engine surfaces from corrosion when the engine is idle.

Yes, there's a big difference in motor oils because there's a big difference in the way they're made. And Conoco Super Motor Oil, proved in famous 50,000-mile road tests—actually *exceeds* the requirements of any car on the road today!

So be good to your car—put Conoco Super Motor Oil in the crankcase!

©1953,
Continental Oil Co.,
Houston, Texas

Saturday Evening Post (August 15, 1953).

96

"Today, some heavy-duty motor oils offer you protection against <u>friction</u> wear.... others offer protection against <u>acid</u> wear. Now Continental Oil Company is proud to announce America's first <u>Double-Duty</u> motor oil.... a new oil that combines two exclusive discoveries (Oil-Plating® and Acid-Proofing)* to protect your car against <u>both</u> friction <u>and</u> acid, the major causes of engine wear."

L. F. McCollum
PRESIDENT, CONTINENTAL OIL COMPANY

Here's why your car needs this great new Double-Duty oil

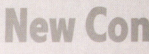

New Conoco Super Motor Oil

America's first Double-Duty* motor oil

is big advertisement will take your *Super* sales story into more than 8,200,000 homes in the SATURDAY EVENING POST of June 12, and COLLIER'S of June 25

Centerfold of *The Red Triangle Magazine* (May-June 1954).

Saturday Evening Post (1953).

Back cover of *The Red Triangle Magazine* (July-August 1954).

Back cover of *The Red Triangle Magazine* (December 1953).

Shooting the Chute

AT 600 M.P.H.

1. Streaking across the sky at near-supersonic speed, the jet fighter bursts into flames. "Bailing out" in the ordinary way is impossible because of extreme air pressures. But, thanks to the newest U.S. Navy safety development, the pilot of a modern jet simply trips a trigger in the cockpit . . . and two exploding cartridges shoot him, seat, parachute and all, out of the blazing airplane to safety.

2. **The exploding escape seat** is an amazing example of a scientific device designed to do the "impossible" . . . just as the amazing new Conoco Super Motor Oil has been scientifically "engineered" to *fight* wear in the engine of your car. New Conoco Super Oil-Plates your engine . . . to make it last longer, perform better, use less gasoline and oil.

3. **50,000 Miles—No Wear!** After a rugged 50,000-mile road-test, engines lubricated with new Conoco Super Motor Oil showed *no wear of any consequence* . . . an average of less than one one-thousandth inch on cylinders and crankshafts! This test also proved that—with proper crankcase drains and regular care—Conoco Super Motor Oil can give you amazing economy. Average gasoline mileage for the last 5,000 miles was actually 99.77% as good as for the first 5,000 miles.

CONOCO Super MOTOR OIL

CONOCO

CONTINENTAL OIL COMPANY, pioneer in oil-perfecting additives, and for over 25 years a leader in oil research, has more than 100 patents on discoveries that improve performance and lengthen the life of your car.

© 1950 **CONTINENTAL OIL COMPANY**

Saturday Evening Post (1950).

Subway in the Sky!

1. **Commuters in Los Angeles** soon may rush to work by this monorail overhead transit system, unhampered by street level traffic. Super-streamlined 100-passenger cars can travel safely at speeds up to 100 miles an hour. The 44-mile run through metropolitan Los Angeles will cut the present commuting time in half.

2. **Better transportation** is a major concern of engineers today. One important way engineers have helped improve transportation by car is the development of Conoco Super Motor Oil, the amazing lubricant that makes engines last longer, perform better, and use less gasoline. This great new oil, with "additives" that "subtract" from engine wear, is now sold coast-to-coast!

3. **50,000 Miles — No Wear!** After a punishing 50,000-mile road test, *with proper drains and regular care,* engines lubricated with Conoco Super Motor Oil showed *no wear of any consequence:* an average of less than one one-thousandth of an inch on cylinders and crankshafts. Gasoline mileage for the last 5,000 miles was actually 99.77% as good as for the first 5,000. Proof that Conoco Super, with Oil-Plating, *helps keep new cars new!*

CAR OWNERS! Your car deserves '50,000 Miles—No Wear' protection and service! Insist on it! Conoco Super is a **heavy duty** oil, now sold coast-to-coast by Continental Oil Company, pioneers in petroleum since 1875 ... and through many progressive distributors, service stations, car dealers, and garages.

DEALERS! Feature Conoco Super as *your* premium motor oil. Your customers will appreciate its engine-protecting high quality!

© 1953 CONTINENTAL OIL COMPANY, HOUSTON, TEXAS   **CONOCO**

Saturday Evening Post (February 28, 1953).

"BAH! NEXT TIME I'LL GET CONOCO BRONZE!"

Switch to Conoco Bronze, Mr. Jobber, Before Your Customers Go Elsewhere for It!

If any customer of your own or your dealers' stations has a tough time starting his car one of these cold mornings . . . and then has to hang on to the choke for blocks . . . *look out!* He'll be heading for a Conoco Bronze pump because he knows (Conoco advertising in newspapers everywhere has told him!) he'll get *instant starting* and *lightning pick-up* in any weather with this high-test gasoline.

Don't *lose* customers—*hold* old customers

and *gain* new ones with Conoco Bronze High-Test Gasoline. It starts cars at zero or 'way below. It improves pick-up. It is high anti-knock, and it gives long mileage.

Conoco Bronze High-Test Gasoline has built astounding sales increases for Conoco jobbers and dealers. Let us tell you how Conoco Bronze, with Conoco's new merchandising plan behind it, can build sales for you. Wire or write us right now that you want a representative to call on you.

CONTINENTAL OIL COMPANY

DIVISION OFFICES

Albuquerque, N. M.
Butte, Mont.
Chicago (Conoco Oil Co.)
Denver, Colo.
Fort Worth, Texas
Great Falls, Montana
Kansas City, Mo.
Lincoln, Neb.
New York, N. Y.
Ponca City, Okla.
Richmond, Va.
Salt Lake City, Utah

THE "INSTANT-STARTING, LIGHTNING PICK-UP" GASOLINE

Unknown publication (November 29, 1933).

Back Cover of *The Red Triangle Magazine* (May-June 1959)

THE TANK TRUCK

Henry Ungersma, left, and Sam Karp, partners in a huge Montana ranching operation, use Conoco Super Motor Oil for all their farming machinery.

Typical of the high standards of farming operation maintained by the Messrs. Ungersma and Karp is this fine flock of New Hampshire Reds.

How to Save $500 a Year

IN MANHATTAN ... whether it's New York, Kansas, Illinois, Nevada or Montana ... saving money is becoming more and more important to everybody. Out near the Montana Manhattan, two big-scale farmers (they raised 60,000 bushels of wheat and 2,500 bushels of peas last year) have found a new way to economize. Won't you let Henry Ungersma and Sam Karp tell you about it?

We have farmed all our lives — the last 20 years for ourselves. Since 1940, we have used Conoco Products in all our equipment with most satisfactory results.

We have lengthened our overhaul periods to three years instead of one year, as previously followed—resulting in a saving to us of approximately $500 per year.

We have always found Conoco Super Motor Oil doing a real job in keeping motors clean, rings free, good compression and producing less consumption of oil. Very little, if any, Conoco Super is added between drains...much less than we experienced with other well-advertised brands.

We have always received most prompt, courteous and efficient service from your Conoco Agent, Hubert G. Fonk, of Manhattan, and your Conoco Jobber, Joe Danhof, of Amsterdam.

Henry Ungersma
Sam Karp

Boston Baked Tomatoes

... by Mrs. Gianna Vaughn
Arkansas City, Kansas

6 large tomatoes   1 can oven-baked beans
2 green peppers, chopped   Salt and pepper
6 slices bacon, diced

Scald and peel the tomatoes. Cut slice from top of each tomato, scooping out the inside. Sauté green peppers and bacon until slightly brown. Add oven-baked beans and drained pulp from tomatoes to peppers and bacon. Season tomato shells with salt and pepper to suit taste. Fill tomato shells with bean mixture. Bake in moderate oven (325 degrees F.) for 20 minutes.

Send your favorite recipes to Mrs. Annie Lee Wheeler, Dep't B, Conoco Cafeteria, Ponca City, Okla. A $7.50 pair of Wiss Pinking Shears awarded for every recipe published with your name. All recipes become property of Continental Oil Company.

FARM KITCHEN

Gives Full Credit to Conoco Super

"In my business of raising cattle and farming," says Rancher H. A. Hartlage, Rosenberg, Texas, "we have to get the most out of an automobile. Conoco Super Motor Oil is used in all the equipment I use to take care of my 500-acre ranch, and I give full credit to Conoco Super for the excellent performance I get out of each piece of farm equipment."

"50,000 Miles-No Wear"

After a punishing 50,000-mile road test, with proper crankcase drains and regular care, engines lubricated with new Conoco Super Motor Oil showed no wear of any consequence . . . in fact, an average of less than one one-thousandth inch on cylinders and crankshafts.

AND gasoline mileage for the last 5,000 miles was actually 99.77% as good as for the first 5,000! This test proved that new Conoco Super with Oil-Plating, can make your cars and trucks last longer, perform better, use less gasoline and oil.

No Mud Holes Now

Make portable hog waterer by mounting large tank on wheel skids and hinging ramp on rear, leading to automatic trough. "No mud holes!" says Nels Thompson, Eagle Grove, Iowa.

No-Sag Hinge

Tighten loose barn-door hinges permanently by welding one end of hinge to strap iron and bolting strap iron to the door frame, suggests Earl Shilling, Scotia, Nebraska.

SAWS FOR IDEAS!

Send your original ideas to The Tank Truck, Dep't B, Continental Oil Company, Ponca City, Okla., and get a genuine $10.25 D-15 Henry Disston Hand Saw for every idea that's printed!

CONOCO

YOUR CONOCO MAN

Farm and Ranch - Southern Agriculturist (June 1951).

No soup! Resisting attempts of man and beast to turn him into soup, the turtle enjoys the *added protection* of his bonelike shell!

Soup, suntan and cider!

No burn! While on the beach your skin gradually builds up a most effective defense against the burning power of the sun by *adding the protection* of extra pigment . . . tan, to you!

No cider! Likewise, the apple does *not* give cider on the limb, because a film of wax seals up the skin . . . gives *added protection*, keeps out air and wild yeast that would ferment the apple's juice.

By *adding* shell, or tan, or wax, Nature protects her own.

And by *adding* a synthetic substance (very like the apple's protective added wax) to Conoco N*th* Motor Oil . . . the *"insides"* of your automobile engine are *extra* protected from costly wear!

This patented substance . . . developed and perfected in Continental's great research laboratories . . . fastens an *extra* film of lubricant so closely to metal that cylinder walls are "OIL-PLATED"! Because "OIL-PLATING" defies gravity . . . won't all drain down, even overnight . . . Conoco N*th* Motor Oil extra-protects you from "dry-friction" starts, from metal-eating combustion acids, from sludge and carbon caused by wear.

For more than a quarter of a century, our main research project has been the application of new knowledge for *your* benefit. Recognized as the pioneer in the use of synthetic "additives" that improve the "oiliness" and metal protective qualities of motor oils, Continental will *keep* ahead by applying every *proven* discovery to one end: *the more efficient, more economical performance of your motor car.*

CONOCO

CONTINENTAL OIL COMPANY

Saturday Evening Post (June 5, 1948).

Down "Suicide 6", Vermont's famed slope, wax can make the difference between a record run and an also ran. Skiers give skis, and their records, the *extra protection* of the right kind of ski wax.

Skis, jellies and cheese!

If you live in the country, you'll find every girl and her mother appreciates the *extra protection* of wax . . . not only in sealing up delicious home-made jams and jellies but in hundreds of other ways.

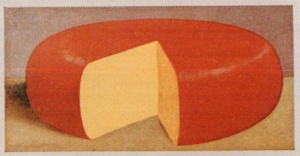

To prevent injury, contamination or spoilage caused by oxidation or moulding, many of your favorite cheeses, fruits and other foods are given the *extra protection* of films of wax, by man or nature.

Now, wax is removed in the manufacturing of highly-refined Conoco Nth Motor Oil . . . *but from this extracted wax, Continental's scientists chemically derive a liquid, oily synthetic compound that helps keep your engine clean* . . .

Added to Nth Oil, this and other synthetic ingredients extra-protect from metal-eating com-

bustion acids . . . from power-clogging sludge . . . from sticky "lacquer" and "varnish."

Since 1922, Continental's main laboratory research project has been the developing of *synthetic* "additives" to improve the lubricating and metal-protective qualities of motor oils. To-day, the practical application of this knowl-

edge for your benefit is indicated by the granting to Continental and its engineers of 109 patents on synthetic "additives" alone. Recognized as the pioneer in this field, Continental will continue to keep ahead by applying every *proven* discovery to one end: *the more efficient, more economical performance of your motor car.*

CONOCO

Copyright 1948, Continental Oil Company

CONTINENTAL OIL COMPANY

Back cover of *The Red Triangle Magazine* (November-December 1948).

As soon as Conoco's Hottest Brand Going contest ends May 15th, this prize-winning poster will begin doing its great selling job for you again. It will remain on all outdoor billboards until June 30th.

Centerfold of *The Red Triangle Magazine* (March-April 1958).

and there were more...

Conoco's prize-winning poster has since had two partners join the campaign and one of these — the cowboy lighting the cigarette — was good enough to take honorable mention in the same Chicago Art Directors contest. Both of them carry out the Hottest Brand Going theme which is aimed at making every year the Hottest Profit Year *ever* for all Conoco dealers.

The Red Triangle Magazine (March-April 1958).

Today–put your car and your cares in **CONOCO'S** hands...

and you'll see why Conoco is the

Hottest Brand Going !

These are the hands that can make you a more confident driver! These are hands you can trust—for service that goes beyond routine —for products that give you an extra measure of value.

Along broad highways and home-town streets, thousands of Conoco hands are taking the cares out of motoring. They extend a friendly welcome to you at the sign of the Red Triangle. It's their skill that makes Conoco the Hottest Brand Going.

STARTING WITH —— FULL COLOR ADVERTISEMENTS **IN** LOOK SAT. EVE. POST **and** LOCAL NEWSPAPERS **in many sizes**

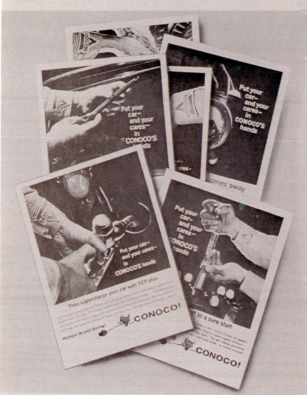

EVERY WEEK This highly popular nighttime television show has proved its sales effectiveness in Conoco-land. Sparkling new "hands" commercials are featured in this season's intensive drive.

RADIO Day and night announcements before and after the most-listened-to programs sell your products and your services forcefully, convincingly, and frequently.

OUTDOOR POSTERS More sales impact for you from dramatic new versions of the "Hottest Brand Going."

FOLLOWED BY: A CONSISTENT SERIES OF FULL COLOR PAGES **IN** LOOK SAT. EVE. POST **and** LOCAL NEWSPAPERS in many sizes

CONTINUING ON: TELEVISION RADIO OUTDOOR POSTERS

In the home and on the road, your advertising-promotional program is working for you . . . reaching 5 out of 6 of your car-owning neighbors over and over again throughout April, May and June . . . bringing a steady flow of traffic to your pumps and to your service bays.

Fold out insert from *The Red Triangle Magazine* (Spring 1960).

Life (1961).

Saturday Evening Post (1960).

Over the past few years, the world of oil and gas collecting has become much smaller. Several monthly publications have come onto the scene devoted strictly to collecting. These publications have made it much more convenient for collectors to trade and communicate together. If you would like information about some of these publications, feel free to contact them at the addresses below and please mention where you heard about them.

> *Matt & Jeff's Oil & Gas Gazette*
> 1000 32nd Street
> Bellingham, WA 98225
>
> *"Check The Oil"*
> P.O. Box 937
> Powell, OH 43065-0937
>
> *Mobilia*
> P.O. Box 575
> Middlebury, VT 05753-9904

There has also been a healthy increase in reference books published on oil and gas collectibles over the past few years. Several are available for those collectors who wish to specialize in one type of memorabilia (i.e. globes, cans, etc.). I highly recommend reading these books before jumping in wallet-first to collecting.

A quarterly price guide is published by Heuser's for the Ertl, Spec-Cast, and Scale Models banks. These price guides are available from your local bank dealer.

In addition to the above publications, there are also several national swap meets devoted exclusively to oil and gas memorabilia. Two that are noteworthy are "Iowa Gas" in Des Moines, Iowa, and the Petroliana Collector's Convention in Columbus, Ohio. For information, write:

> Iowa Gas Swap Meet, Inc.
> 4420-96th Ct.
> Des Moines, Iowa 50322
>
> "CTO!"
> P.O. Box 937
> Powell, Ohio 43065-0937

BIBLIOGRAPHY

Conoco Germ Processed Motor Oil." *Continental Oil Company Service Manual*, 1936, 26-29.

Conoco: The First One Hundred Years. New York: Dell Publishing Co., Inc. 1975.

Conoco Travel Bureau and Passport Service, brochure, 1934.

"Destruction in Death Valley." *The Red Triangle Magazine*, May-June 1941, 10-17.

"Now...In Sealed Cans." *The Red Triangle Magazine*, May 1937, 2-3.

Proved by a Daring Destruction Test, brochure, 1932.

We're Breaking Ground for Another 75 Years, brochure, 1950.